where do they go?

where do they go?

JULIA ALVAREZ

illustrated by
SABRA FIELD

SEVEN STORIES 7

TRIANGLE SQUARE
books for young readers

NEW YORK • OAKLAND

When somebody dies,
where do they go?

Who can I ask?
Does anyone know?

Do they go where the wind goes
when it blows?

Do
they
turn
into
clouds

and change
every
hour:

a flamingo,
a cat,
a dancer,
a flower?

Do they dive into rivers and dissolve in the sea?
Do they tickle my feet when waves wash over me?

Do they drift with the snow?
Are they sad? Are they cold?

Can I catch them as snowflakes on the tip of my tongue?
Are they that quiet feeling at the end of a song?

Do they wink back at me
    when I wish on a star?
Do they whisper,
    "You're perfect, just as you are"?

Do they listen to secrets?
Do they nod when I ask
    for help with a specially
    difficult task?

Do they grow wings when they die and fly far away?
Or hover above me when I need them to stay?

Will they answer my questions?
Will they still hold my hand?
Will they say not to worry
if I don't understand?

Is it them that I feel,
alive in my heart?
Is it there that I go when
I'm sad we're apart?

Are they hiding on rooftops,
at the foot of the stairs,

so I'll stop and look closely
to search for them there?

in the sun as it sets when the long day is done,
in the waves as they roll on the sea on and on.

Sometimes very briefly, I catch just a glance
in the hills' quiet stillness, in a storm's dark advance.

Just a glimpse, just a peek, a small puzzle I solve
when I'm loving the world they left me to love.